Staying Healthy

by Addie N. Weiller

PEARSON
Scott
Foresman

What You Already Know

Your body's organs do many important jobs. These include taking in food and oxygen, getting rid of waste, and moving all these materials around. This work is done by the digestive, respiratory, urinary, and circulatory systems.

The center of the circulatory system is the heart. It works non-stop to pump blood around your body. The heart contains valves that keep blood flowing in the right direction. The blood travels through blood vessels, or tubes, called arteries, veins, and capillaries. Blood is made up of red cells, which carry oxygen, white cells, which fight disease, and platelets, which heal wounds.

The respiratory system takes oxygen from the air and transfers it into the blood, which takes it to your cells. The nose, mouth, trachea, bronchial tubes, mucus, and lungs are all parts of the respiratory system. Inside the lungs, oxygen enters the blood and waste gases such as carbon dioxide leave it. The respiratory system is powered by the diaphragm, a large muscle that does all the work of breathing.

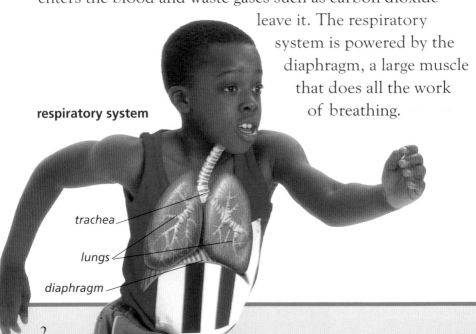

respiratory system

trachea

lungs

diaphragm

The digestive system brings food into the body and gets rid of waste. It starts when you put food in your mouth and swallow it down your esophagus. The food travels through your stomach and small intestine. It gets broken into smaller and smaller pieces as it goes along. Nutrients get absorbed through the walls of the small intestine and are passed into the blood, which carries them to the cells. The digested food then goes into the large intestine and out of the body.

The urinary system filters waste out of the blood. Each cell sends its waste into the bloodstream, which takes it to the kidneys. They filter out the waste and excess water. This material then leaves the body.

esophagus

liver

stomach

large instestine

small instestine

Your body is very complicated. All of these systems, as well as several others, need to be taken care of. What can you do to treat your body right? You'll find out in this book.

Introduction

How do you feel? Do you have plenty of energy? Do you ever get sick? Is your body always ready to do the things you need it to do? If you want to stay healthy, you need to take care of yourself.

To stay healthy, there are a few things you should do. Don't worry, though, none of them are very hard. In fact, you probably do some of these things already. Taking care of your body is easy and it will make you feel good. Even better, it can be fun!

Keeping yourself healthy is all about giving your body what it needs. What your body needs is a healthy diet, exercise, regular cleaning, and the right amount of sleep. Your diet gives you energy and helps you grow. Exercise turns your energy into strong bones and muscles. Staying clean helps keep you from getting sick. Sleeping gives your body and mind a chance to rest and repair themselves.

So what do you have to do to take care of these needs? Let's find out!

Healthy Eating

The first thing you need for good health is good food. Food does two important jobs. First, it gives you the material your body needs to grow. Second, it gives you the energy you need to move, think, breathe, and everything else you need to do in life. If you want your body to be made from the best material, and you want all the energy you can get, you need to choose your food carefully. But how can you know what you should eat?

Fruits are good for you—they are low in fat and high in vitamins.

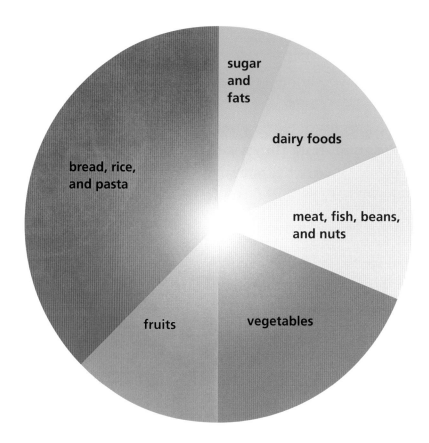

This pie chart can help you remember how much of each food to eat.

Charts like the one above are an easy way to keep track of what you should be eating. This one is a pie chart, since its sections are shaped like slices of a pie. Each section represents a type of food. Foods you should eat lots of, such as bread and grains, get a large slice of the pie. Foods you should eat less of, such as sugar and fats, get a smaller slice. Fruits, vegetables, meats, and dairy foods all get medium-sized slices. The chart doesn't tell you exactly how much of each food you should eat, but it gives you an idea of what portion of your diet should be made up of each type of food.

So now you know what to eat and how much, but what are you getting from all this food? Well, some of the most important things food gives you are carbohydrates. You may have heard them called "carbs" or "carbos." Carbohydrates are what your body uses to make energy. There are two types of carbs: simple and complex. Simple carbohydrates are better known as sugars. Complex carbohydrates are usually called starches. They are found in foods such as bread and potatoes.

pasta

vegetable soup

Orange juice contains vitamin C, which may help keep you from getting sick.

Your food also provides you with protein. Protein is found in meat, chicken, fish, eggs, dairy products, nuts, and beans. Protein helps you out in a very big way: it builds and repairs your body. Your muscles and organs are made up almost completely of protein. It helps your blood carry oxygen. Protein also helps fight disease and heal cuts.

Vitamins and minerals also come from food. Your body needs them to do many jobs. For example, calcium is a mineral that makes your teeth and bones strong. Vitamin C protects you from illness. Vitamins and minerals do hundreds of other jobs too.

Your body doesn't run on food alone. You also need water. Without it, you wouldn't survive for more than a few days. Water makes up most of your blood. It helps food move through your body, and it keeps you cool by forming sweat. So drink lots of water!

Living with Diabetes

Diabetes is a disease that people get when an organ called the pancreas stops working correctly. When this happens, you end up with too much sugar in your blood. This can lead to problems with the heart, eyes, kidneys, nerves, and teeth. One kind of diabetes may be avoided by eating right and exercising. This boy is checking his blood sugar.

Keeping Fit

You've heard your parents say it before: "Turn off that TV and go play outside!" But why? Are they worried you're wearing out the couch? Actually, your parents know that everybody needs exercise, even kids.

So what can exercise do for you? First of all, it's good for your heart. Doing aerobic exercise will help to make your heart stronger. Aerobic exercises are the kind that bring lots of oxygen to your muscles and really get your heart pumping. When your heart is stronger, you can do more without getting tired.

Exercising also helps keep you from getting overweight. If you just sit in front of a TV or computer screen all day, you may find yourself putting on the pounds. Weighing too much can lead to many different health problems later in life. Plus, it makes it harder to move around and be active.

Flexibility is another good thing that comes from exercise. Maybe touching your toes isn't very important to you, but being flexible can help keep you safe. If you are more flexible, you're less likely to get hurt when you're playing sports or games.

When you think about exercise, you might picture people with huge muscles. But building strong muscles doesn't have to mean looking like a cartoon superhero. Being stronger can help you with everything from riding your bike to doing chores. When your muscles are in good shape, it makes any hard work easier.

The great thing about exercise is that anyone can find a type they like. Look at the kids on these pages. Are any of them doing something you like to do? Or is there a kind of exercise you like that's not shown? Let's look at different kinds of exercise, and how each one can help you stay healthy.

Playing soccer is a good way to increase your stamina. It's an aerobic exercise. Cycling is also good for stamina, and it builds strong leg muscles.

Tennis helps with your coordination. Dancing can improve your balance, and it also builds muscle.

Any of these activities is a good way to stay fit. The important thing when choosing a sport or other exercise is to pick one you like. That way, you're more likely to stick with it.

Exercise Benefits

Toning muscles

Stamina

Balance

Coordination

Strength

Body Basics

Keeping Clean

You've built a strong body by eating right and exercising. So that's all you have to do, right? Well, not quite. You have to take care of that body you've worked so hard on. How? First, you have to keep clean.

Washing your hands helps to protect you from germs.

An important part of keeping clean is washing your hands. Think of all the things you touch in a day. Maybe you spent a science class studying live frogs. Did you help clean up the lunch table? Or maybe you played with a dirty basketball during recess.

Doing any of these things exposes you to germs. Germs are tiny living things that can make you sick. Luckily, washing your hands can help keep you safe from germs. The first step is to reach for the soap. It doesn't matter what kind you use, so pick one you like. Next, run some warm water. Now start scrubbing! Wash your wrists, both sides of your hands, and especially around your fingernails. You should spend between ten and fifteen seconds scrubbing. When you're done, make sure to dry your hands on a clean towel.

There's more to keeping clean than just washing your hands. You have to wash the rest of your body too. Dirt and oil can irritate your skin if you don't wash them off. Taking a bath or a shower every day will make you look better and feel clean. While you're at it, remember to wash your hair and face.

Hand soap and shampoo are important tools for keeping yourself clean.

Your teeth are very important. You use them to eat your food, and your smile just wouldn't look the same without them. You should protect them from their worst enemy: sugar!

Tiny life forms called bacteria like sugar as much as you do! When bacteria find sugar on your teeth, they change it into acid. This acid makes holes, called cavities, in teeth. Bacteria also cause other problems, like gum disease. The sticky stuff that holds bacteria and sugar on your teeth is plaque.

You should spend at least three minutes every time you brush your teeth.

To keep your teeth free of cavities and plaque, you have to brush them with some toothpaste and a toothbrush. Make sure your toothpaste contains fluoride, which helps fight cavities. Choose a toothbrush with soft bristles, and get a new one every three months. Brush at least twice a day, once after breakfast and once before bed.

It is also a good idea to floss your teeth. Flossing cleans the spaces between your teeth, which your toothbrush can't reach.

Another way to protect your teeth is to go to the dentist twice a year. Dentists check to make sure you don't have cavities or gum disease. They also give your teeth a super cleaning.

If you have very crooked teeth, your dentist might give you braces. These are metal wires that slowly move your teeth into the right places.

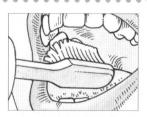

1. Brush away from your gums.

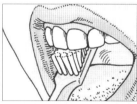

2. Make sure to brush both the back and front of each tooth.

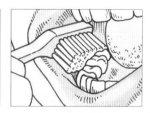

3. Don't forget to brush all your teeth, even the ones way in the back.

Eyes and Ears

Do you know anyone who wears glasses? Some people need them because they are either nearsighted or farsighted. To someone who is nearsighted, things far away are blurry. A farsighted person has difficulty seeing things that are close up.

If you think you might have one of these problems, you might want to go to the doctor to get an eye test. Then the doctor might give you glasses or contact lenses to correct your vision.

Your ears need to be treated right too. You should never stick anything in your ears, even cotton swabs. This can lead to damage or an ear infection. Ear infections are also caused when water gets stuck in your ear. You should always make sure to dry your ears after swimming.

eye test chart

Hearing Problems

Sometimes people lose their hearing due to disease, head injuries, or very bad ear infections. This hearing loss can be treated with medicine or operations. If neither of these help, a person might have to wear a hearing aid.

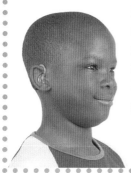 Hearing aids are like tiny speakers that make sounds louder inside your ear.

Your ears can also be hurt by loud noises. This is why construction workers wear ear protectors when they use a jackhammer. Your ears can be damaged by loud music, so be careful not to listen to your headphones too loud. It can lead to hearing loss or a ringing in the ears that never goes away.

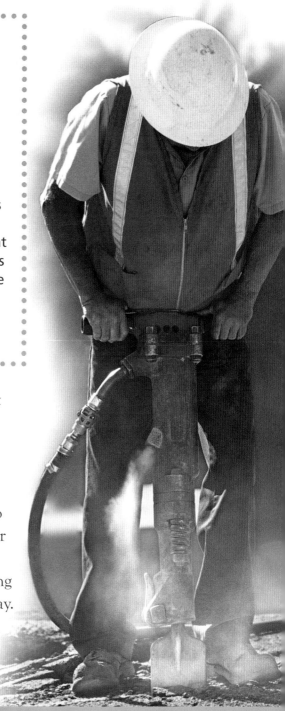

Weather Wise

Imagine lying in the sun at the beach. You may be relaxed, but this is no time to take a vacation from staying healthy! That sunlight feels good on your skin, but it can be bad for your health.

Too much sunlight on your skin can cause skin cancer. This is a very serious disease that doctors have difficulty curing. So be careful in the sun!

When you're out in the sun, try to stay covered by wearing a shirt over your bathing suit. When it's time to go swimming, always wear sunscreen. You should use a sunscreen with an SPF (sun protection factor) of 15 or higher. The sun can also be bad for your eyes. So put on some sunglasses when you're out on a sunny day.

The summer isn't the only time to be careful of the weather. You have to protect yourself from the cold too. Dress in layers to trap warm air next to your body, and always wear a hat. Choose clothing made of wool, down, or fleece. And watch those fingers and toes! These parts of your body get cold very easily. You might want to wear mittens instead of gloves, because they keep your fingers warmer.

When it's cold, your body uses lots of energy just to keep you warm. Help it out by dressing in layers.

Hay Fever

Do you sneeze when you go into a flower shop? You may be allergic to pollen. This allergy is called "hay fever," because many people are allergic to hay. People with hay fever may sneeze, have a runny nose, or have watery eyes. To avoid this allergy, stay inside on dry days when plants are blooming.

Sleep

You've eaten a healthy meal, exercised, taken a shower, and played outside. You must be tired. Time for some rest! But don't feel like you're being lazy just because you lie down for a nap. Sleeping is an important part of staying healthy.

Without sleep, people could not survive. Sleep helps your body fight illness, and it repairs your cells. It also helps you think clearly. And of course, if you don't sleep, you'll be too tired to do anything! You won't be able to concentrate. You'll also be clumsy, and your mood might change for no reason.

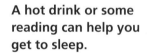

A hot drink or some reading can help you get to sleep.

Stages of Sleep

Stage 1
Your brain tells your muscles to relax. Your heart beats a little slower and your body temperature drops slightly.

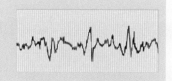

Stage 2
After a while you will be in light sleep. You can be woken up easily during this stage.

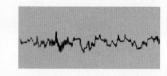

Stage 3
You will be in deeper sleep. Your blood pressure lowers and your body isn't sensitive to the temperature around you.

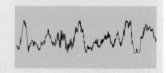

Stage 4
This is the deepest sleep. It is hard to wake up from this stage. Some people may sleepwalk or talk in their sleep.

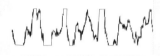

Stage 5
REM (Rapid Eye Movement)—during this stage, the eyes move around quickly. People have most of their dreams during REM sleep. Scientists think this stage helps you to learn and remember.

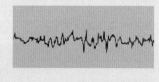

Staying healthy takes a little work, but it's worth it. If you take care of yourself, you'll get sick less, have more energy, and feel great. And you can have fun doing it!

Glossary

aerobic exercise	exercise that makes the heart pump harder and faster, such as jogging or jumping rope
bacteria	tiny life forms that can cause disease
carbohydrates	materials in food that provide energy
diabetes	a disease that keeps the body from controlling the levels of sugar in the blood
fluoride	an ingredient in toothpaste that prevents cavities
plaque	a sticky film found on the teeth
protein	a material found in food that helps build and repair muscles and organs
skin cancer	a disease of the skin that can be caused by too much sunlight
SPF	the level of protection a sunscreen gives from the sun; stands for "sun protection factor"